# SPIN!

## Grammar, Vocabulary, and Writing

B

## Genevieve J. Kocienda

**LONGMAN ON THE WEB**

Longman.com offers online resources for teachers and students. Access our Companion Websites, our online catalog, and our local offices around the world.

Longman English Success offers online courses to give learners flexible study options. Courses cover General English, Business English, and Exam Preparation.

Visit us at longman.com and englishsuccess.com.

Longman

**Spin! B**

Pearson Education, 10 Bank Street, White Plains, NY 10606

Vice president, director of instructional design: Allen Ascher
Executive editor: Anne Stribling
Senior development editor: Virginia Bernard
Vice president, director of design and production: Rhea Banker
Executive managing editor: Linda Moser
Production manager: Liza Pleva
Production editor: Sylvia Dare
Art director: Patricia Wosczyk
Director of manufacturing: Patrice Fraccio
Senior manufacturing buyer: Edith Pullman
Cover design: Elizabeth Carlson
Cover art: Mary Jane Begin
Cover photo: © Getty Images
Text design: Patricia Wosczyk
Text composition: TSI Graphics
Text art: Teresa Anderko

ISBN: 0-13-041985-0

3 4 5 6 7 8 9 10—WC—07 06 05 04 03

# Contents

# Numbers

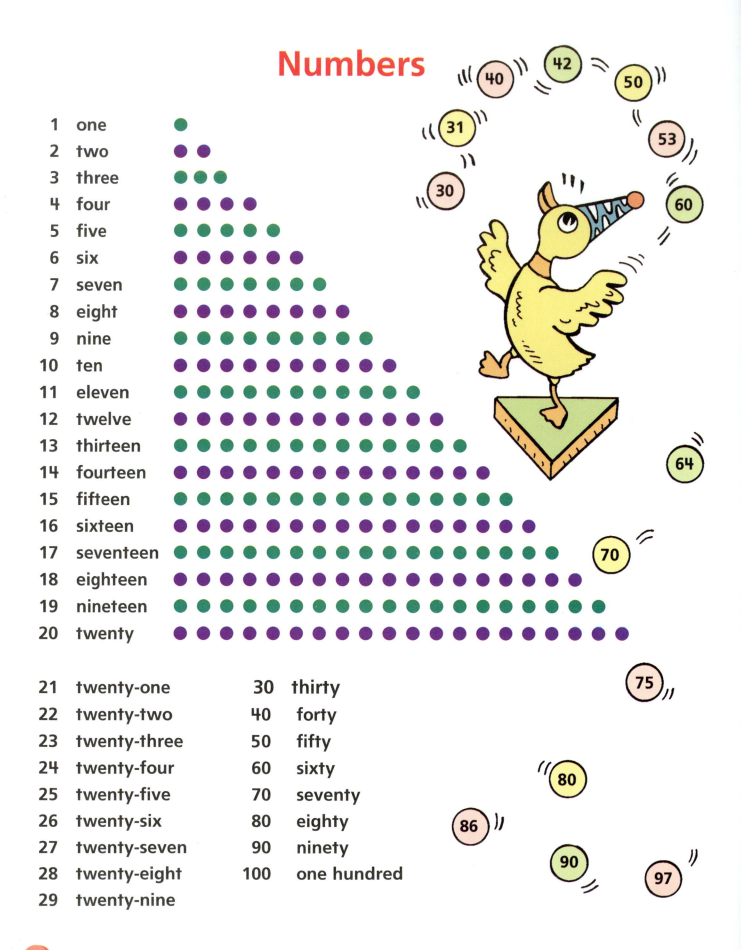

| | |
|---|---|
| 1 one | |
| 2 two | |
| 3 three | |
| 4 four | |
| 5 five | |
| 6 six | |
| 7 seven | |
| 8 eight | |
| 9 nine | |
| 10 ten | |
| 11 eleven | |
| 12 twelve | |
| 13 thirteen | |
| 14 fourteen | |
| 15 fifteen | |
| 16 sixteen | |
| 17 seventeen | |
| 18 eighteen | |
| 19 nineteen | |
| 20 twenty | |

| | | | |
|---|---|---|---|
| 21 | twenty-one | 30 | thirty |
| 22 | twenty-two | 40 | forty |
| 23 | twenty-three | 50 | fifty |
| 24 | twenty-four | 60 | sixty |
| 25 | twenty-five | 70 | seventy |
| 26 | twenty-six | 80 | eighty |
| 27 | twenty-seven | 90 | ninety |
| 28 | twenty-eight | 100 | one hundred |
| 29 | twenty-nine | | |

# Shapes

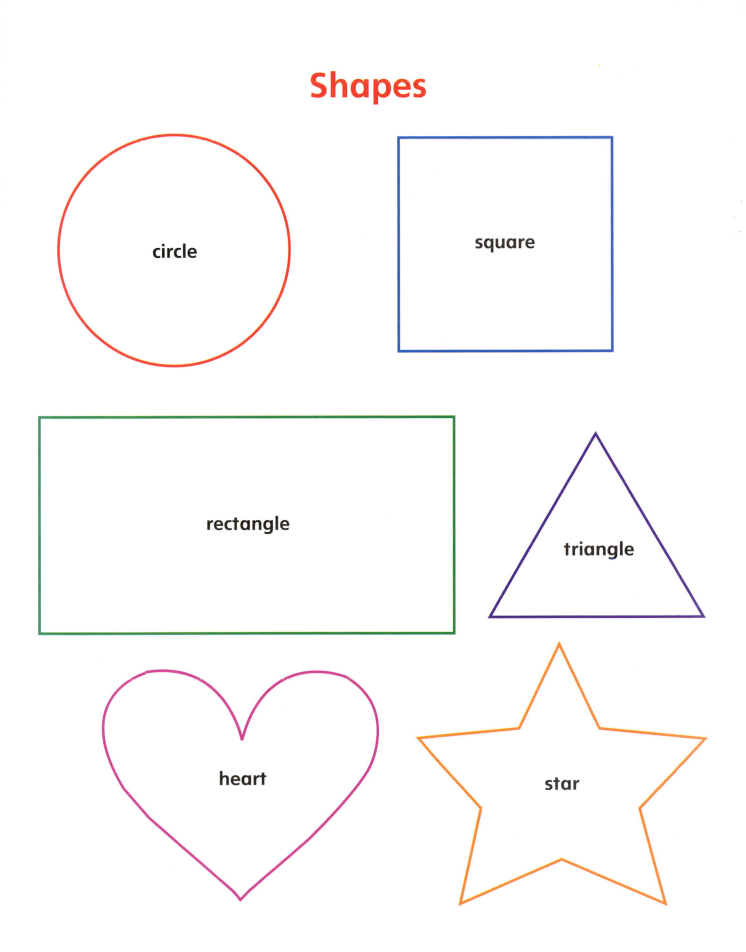

circle

square

rectangle

triangle

heart

star

# Seasons

spring

summer

fall

winter

# Time

**6:00**

six o'clock

**6:05**

six-oh-five

**6:10**

six ten

**6:15**

six fifteen

**6:20**

six twenty

**6:25**

six twenty-five

**6:30**

six thirty

**6:35**

six thirty-five

**6:40**

six forty

**6:45**

six forty-five

**6:50**

six fifty

**6:55**

six fifty-five

# Imperatives

Sit down.

Stand up.

Look at the board.

Open your book.

Close your book.

Raise your hand.

Come here.

Be quiet.

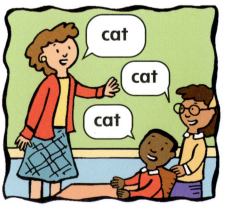
Please repeat.

# Hello!

# My Class

window

door

notebook

glue

scissors

paper

picture

# Contractions

I am = I'm    you are = you're    he is = he's    she is = she's

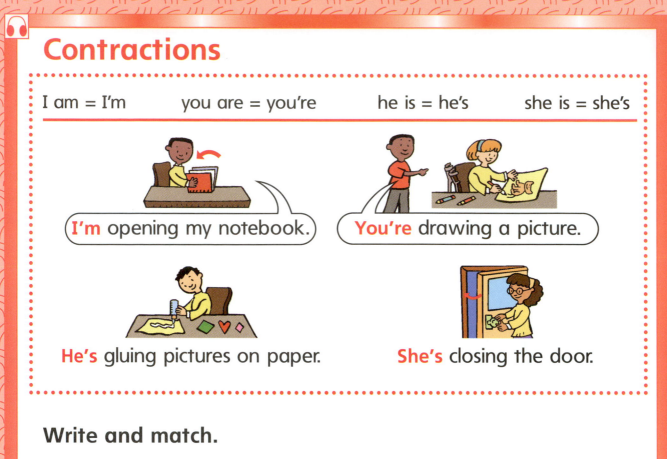

I'm opening my notebook.

You're drawing a picture.

He's gluing pictures on paper.

She's closing the door.

## Write and match.

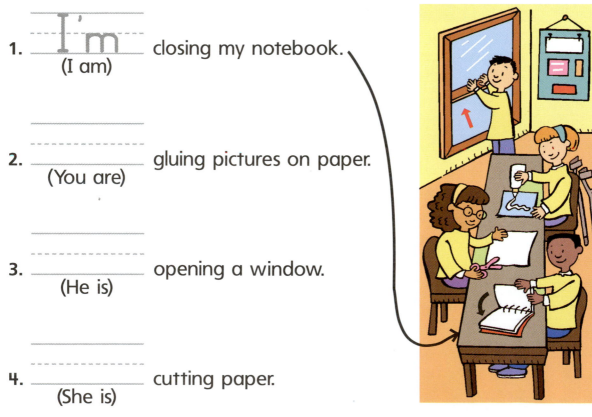

1. I'm _____ closing my notebook.
   (I am)

2. _____ gluing pictures on paper.
   (You are)

3. _____ opening a window.
   (He is)

4. _____ cutting paper.
   (She is)

# Contractions

they are = they're    we are = we're

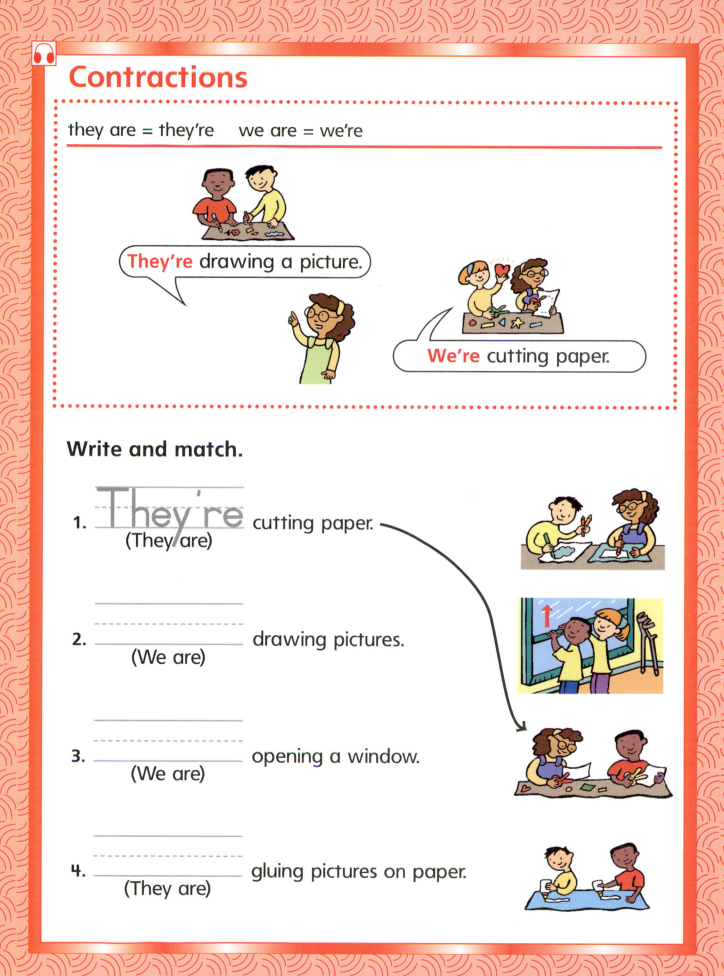

**They're** drawing a picture.

**We're** cutting paper.

## Write and match.

1. They're cutting paper.
(They are)

2. _____ drawing pictures.
(We are)

3. _____ opening a window.
(We are)

4. _____ gluing pictures on paper.
(They are)

**Write and draw.**

1. They are drawing a picture.

They're drawing a picture.

2. I am cutting paper.

3. He is opening the window.

4. She is closing a notebook.

# Irregular Plurals

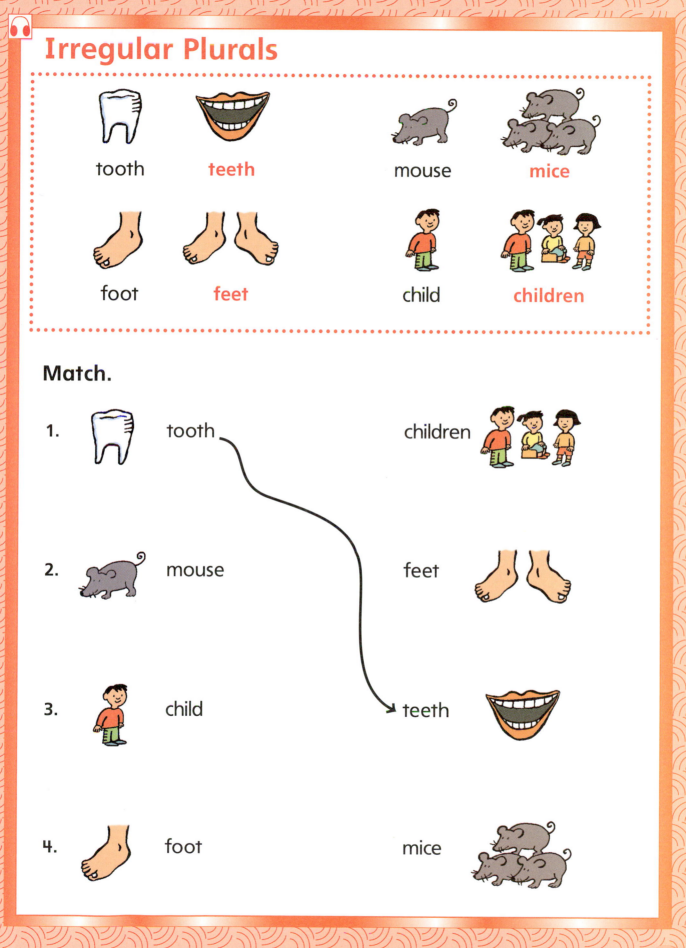

tooth  **teeth**  mouse  **mice**

foot  **feet**  child  **children**

**Match.**

1. tooth        children

2. mouse        feet

3. child        teeth

4. foot        mice

## A. Write.

1. foot     feet

2. child

3. mouse

4. tooth

## B. Circle.

1. They are mouse / mice.

2. This is my foot / feet.

3. He is a child / children.

4. These are tooth / teeth.

 **Chant.**

He's drawing a picture.
He is.
He is.

She's gluing the pictures.
She is.
She is.

You're closing a window.
You are.
You are.

I'm cutting paper.
I am.
I am.

# Find the differences.

**1.**

**2.**

# On the Playground

**UNIT 2**

sun

tree

cloud

squirrel

butterfly

swing

seesaw

bench

flower

ant

# Prepositions: behind, next to, above

The cloud is **behind** the sun.

The cloud is **next to** the sun.

The cloud is **above** the sun.

## Read and draw.

1. The sun is above the cloud.

2. The tree is next to the flower.

3. The butterfly is above the ant.

4. The squirrel is behind the tree.

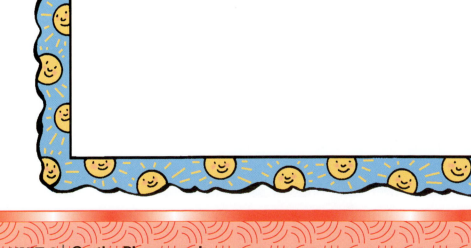

## A. Write.

next to    above    behind

1. The squirrel is **behind** the flower.

2. The butterfly is _____ the seesaw.

3. The ants are _____ the tree.

4. The sun is _____ the cloud.

## B. Unscramble.

1. the / above / butterfly / ants / is / The

**The butterfly is above the ants.**

2. is / the / swing / The / seesaw / behind

_____

3. flower / is / squirrel / next to / The / the

_____

# There is / There are

There **is** a cloud in the sky.

There **are** clouds in the sky.

**Write.**

1. There are flowers behind the bench.

2. _____ a butterfly above the flowers.

3. _____ ants next to the squirrel.

4. _____ a cloud above the sun.

# How many...?

**How many** flowers are there?

There is one flower.

**How many** flowers are there?

There are five flowers.

**Write.**

**1.**

How many trees are there?

There are five trees.

**2.**

There is one sun.

**3.**

There are seven ants.

**4.**

There is one swing.

**Write and draw.**

1. How many squirrels are there?

   There is one squirrel.

2. _____ flowers are there?

   _____ four flowers.

3. _____ clouds are there?

   _____ three clouds.

4. _____ suns are there?

   _____ one sun.

5. _____ ants are there?

   _____ five ants.

There is an ant.
Where's the ant?
The ant is next to the tree.
The ant is next to the tree.

There is a sun.
Where's the sun?
The sun is above the cloud.
The sun is above the cloud.

There is a squirrel.
Where's the squirrel?
The squirrel is behind the bench.
The squirrel is behind the bench.

There is a flower.
Where's the flower?
The flower is next to the swing.
The flower is next to the swing.

# Find the flower.

START

# Review: Units 1 and 2

## Vocabulary

A. Listen and check.

## There is/There are

B. Listen and check.

# Review: Units 1 and 2

## Prepositions

C. Listen and check.

## How many...?

D. Listen, point, and say.

# Our House

# Possessives: my, your

This is **my** house.

That's **your** house.

that's = that is

## Write and match.

1. This is ___my___ computer.

2. That's _____ computer.

3. This is _____ bike.

4. That's _____ bike.

5. This is _____ pet.

# Possessives: -'s

That's Matt**'s** house.

## Write and match.

1. That's _Taro's_ bike.
   (Taro)

2. That's _____ computer.
   (Ana)

3. That's _____ pet.
   (Matt)

4. That's _____ pet.
   (Jen)

5. That's _____ bike.
   (Ana)

## A. Circle.

1. This is (my) / your house.

2. That's **Ana's** / **my** bike.

3. That's **my** / **Matt's** pet.

4. That's **your** / **my** bike.

5. This is **my** / **your** computer.

## B. Point and say.

house

window

rug

sink

telephone

radio

door

# Is there...?/Are there...?

**Is there** a mirror in the house?
Yes, there is.

**Is there** a telephone in the house?
No, there isn't.

**Are there** windows in the house?
Yes, there are.

**Are there** rugs in the house?
No, there aren't.

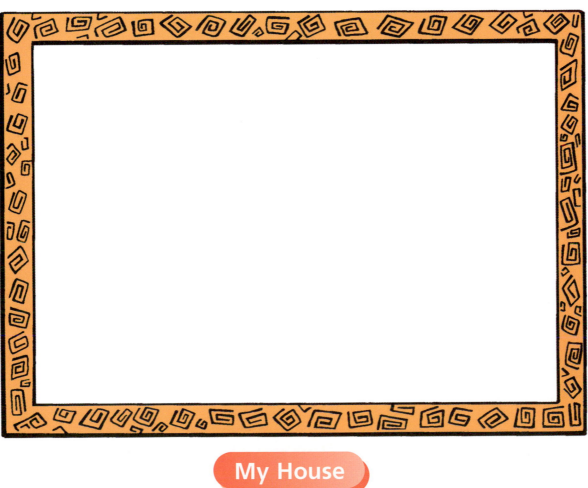

**Draw.**

My House

**Look and write.**

1. Is there a radio in the house?

   Yes, there is.

2. Are there telephones in the house?

3. _____ a sink in the house?

4. _____ mirrors in the house?

5. _____ a computer in the house?

 **Chant.**

Are there rugs in the house?
Yes, there are.
Yes, there are.

Are there mirrors in the house?
No, there aren't.
No, there aren't.

Is there a radio in the house?
Yes, there is.
Yes, there is.

Is there a bike in the house?
No, there isn't.
No, there isn't.

What's wrong?

# My Community

supermarket

hospital

restaurant

Library

library

Supermarket

Hospital

Restaurant

Bank

bank

bookstore

post office

bakery

Bakery

Bookstore

Post Office

Mail

# Prepositions: on, between

The hospital is **on** Green Street.

The hospital is **between** the bank and the post office.

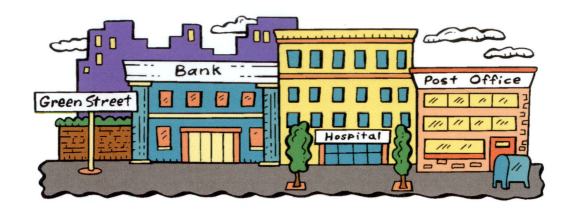

**Look and write.**

1. The bank is **between** the bakery and the restaurant.

2. The hospital is _____ Long Street.

3. The bakery is _____ White Street.

4. The library is _____ the hospital and the bookstore.

# Adjectives

Adjectives describe people, places, or things.

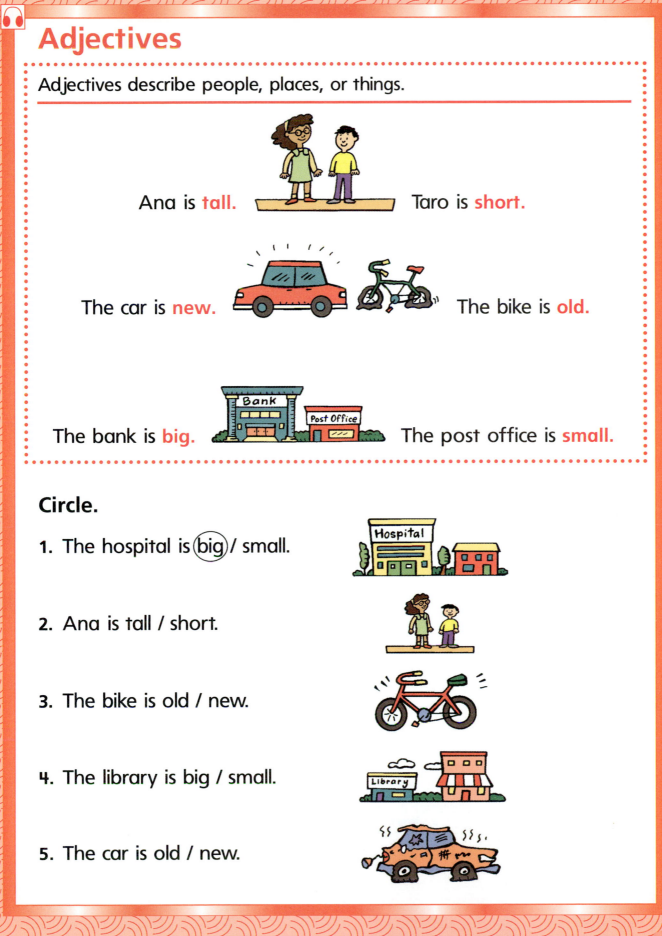

Ana is **tall.**          Taro is **short.**

The car is **new.**          The bike is **old.**

The bank is **big.**          The post office is **small.**

## Circle.

1. The hospital is (big) / small.

2. Ana is tall / short.

3. The bike is old / new.

4. The library is big / small.

5. The car is old / new.

## A. Write.

1. The bank is _____ .
   big / small

2. Taro is _____ .
   tall / short

3. The bike is _____ .
   old / new

4. The ant is _____ .
   big / small

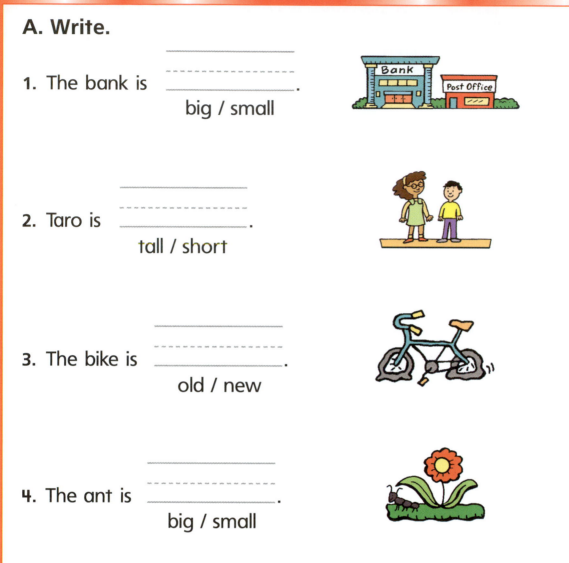

## B. Point and say.

The big bank is **on** Apple Street.

The new hospital is **between** the bakery and the bank.

The small library is **next to** the bakery.

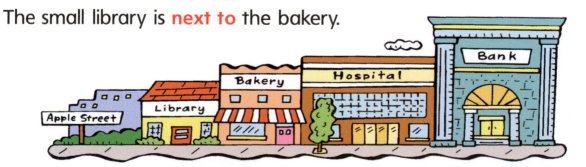

# Proper Nouns

The name of a person or place is a **proper noun.** It is always capitalized.

Do not use *a* or *an* before a proper noun.

It's a street.

It's **White Street.**

**Write.**

1. It's a restaurant. (The Green Frog)

It's The Green Frog.

2. It's a bookstore. (The Old Bookstore)

_____

_____

3. It's a market. (Mike's Market)

_____

_____

4. It's a bakery. (Bill's Bakery)

_____

_____

5. It's a restaurant. (The Red Mango)

_____

_____

**Draw and color.**

My Restaurant

 **Chant.**

The bakery is new.
It's Tom's Bakery.
It's Tom's Bakery.

The restaurant is small.
It's Jo's Restaurant.
It's Jo's Restaurant.

The bookstore is tall.
It's Sam's Bookstore.
It's Sam's Bookstore.

# Review: Units 3 and 4

## Vocabulary

🎧 A. Listen and check.

1.
□  □

2.
□  □

3.
□  □

4.
□  □

## Prepositions

🎧 B. Listen and check.

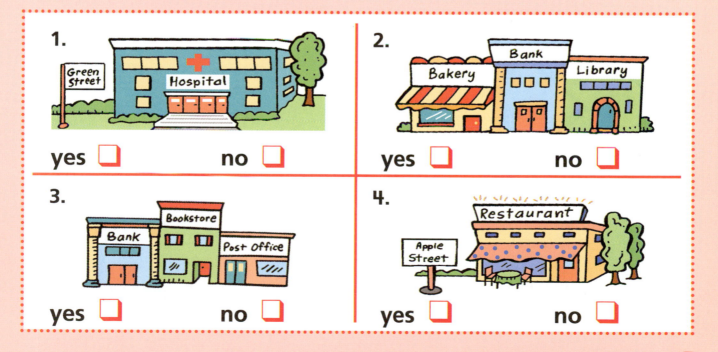

1.
yes □    no □

2.
yes □    no □

3.
yes □    no □

4.
yes □    no □

# Review: Units 3 and 4

## Adjectives

🎧 C. Listen and check.

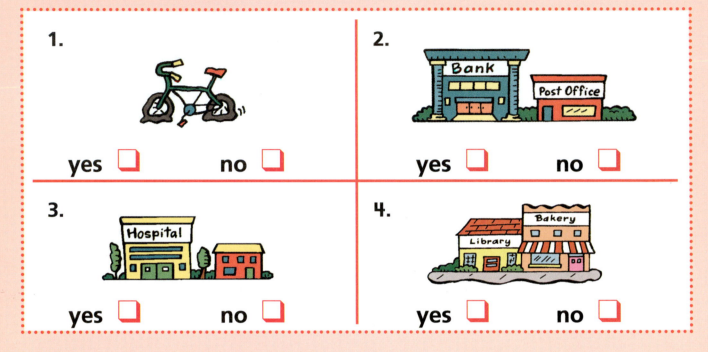

1.
yes ☐   no ☐

2.
yes ☐   no ☐

3.
yes ☐   no ☐

4.
yes ☐   no ☐

## Is there...?/Are there...?

🎧 D. Listen, point, and say.

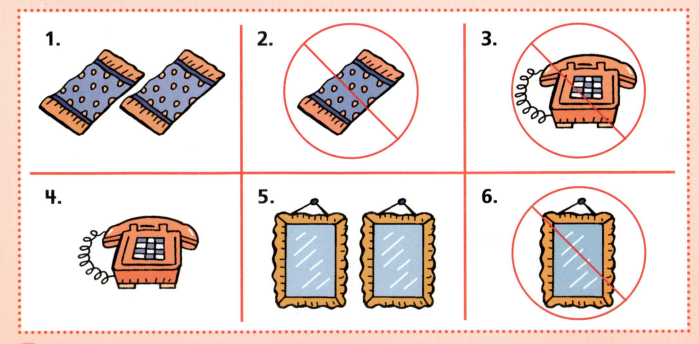

1.   2.   3.
4.   5.   6.

# Workers

Fire Station

Office

Restaurant

clerk

firefighter

cook

Hospital

doctor

dentist

Library

vet

nurse

mail carrier

School

Flowers

librarian

teacher

police officer

# What ...?

**Write.**

1.

## What does she do?

She's a cook.

2.

He's a doctor.

3.

She's a librarian.

4.

He's a teacher.

5.

She's a nurse.

# Who ...?

**Who** is he?

He's Mr. Black.

He's a firefighter.

**Who** is she?

She's Dr. White.

She's a dentist.

## Write.

**1.**

Who is she?

She's Dr. Brown.

She's a vet.

**2.**

He's Mr. Long.

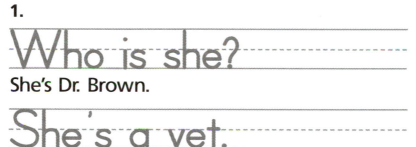

**3.**

She's Mrs. Small.

**Write and match.**

1. What does she do?
   She's a _____ nurse.

2. _____ cook.

3. _____ doctor.

4. _____ dentist.

5. _____ firefighter.

6. _____ clerk.

# Where ...?

Where does a doctor work?

A doctor works in a hospital.

**Write and draw.**

1. A nurse works in a hospital.

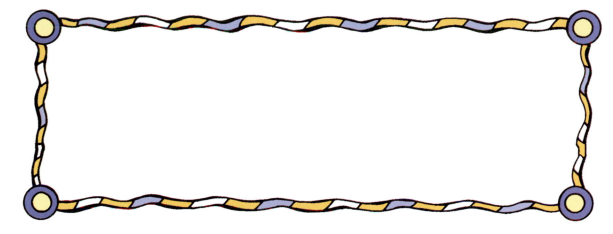

2. A teacher works in a school.

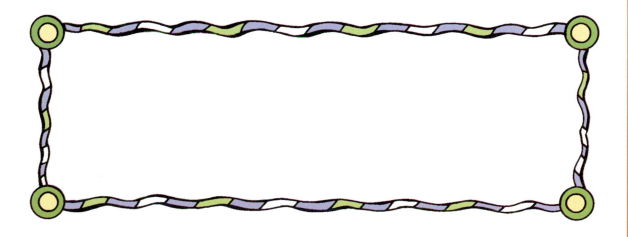

**Write.**

1. Where does a ___nurse___ work?

   A ___nurse___ works in a hospital.

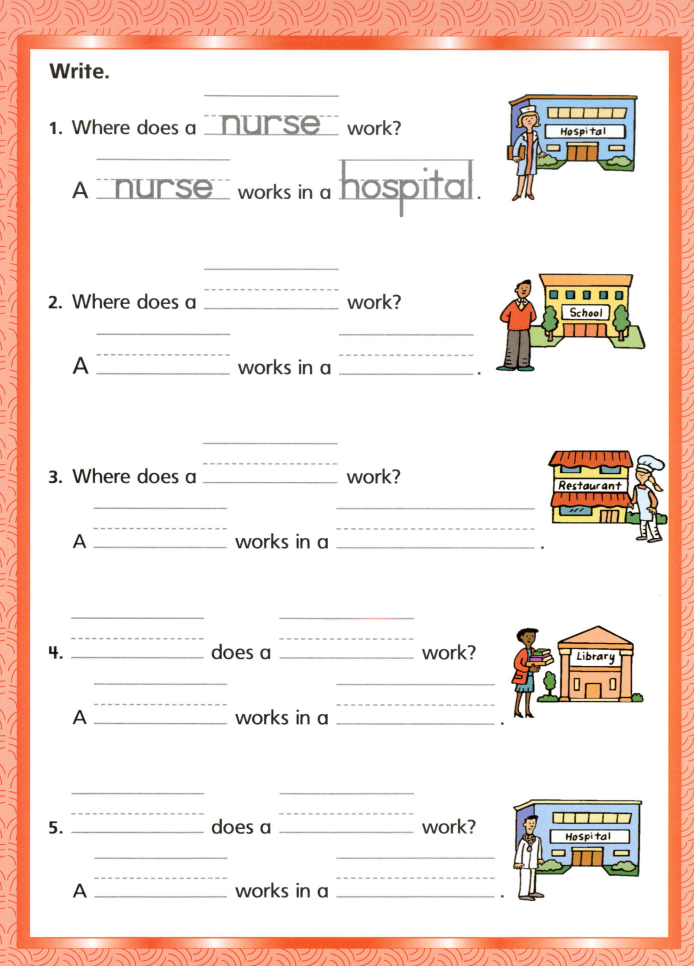

2. Where does a _____ work?

   A _____ works in a _____.

3. Where does a _____ work?

   A _____ works in a _____.

4. _____ does a _____ work?

   A _____ works in a _____.

5. _____ does a _____ work?

   A _____ works in a _____.

 **Chant.**

Dentist, doctor, nurse
Dentist, doctor, nurse

She's a dentist.
She's a dentist.

Dentist, doctor, nurse
Dentist, doctor, nurse

He's a doctor.
He's a doctor.

Dentist, doctor, nurse
Dentist, doctor, nurse

She's a nurse.
She's a nurse.
Dentist, doctor, nurse.

# What ...? Who ...? Where ...?

# My Day

wake up

eat breakfast

get dressed

go to school

eat lunch

go home

play the piano

eat dinner

listen to music

go to sleep

# Simple Present

I **wake up** at 6:00.

I **eat** breakfast at 6:15.

I **get dressed** at 6:30.

I **go** to school at 6:45.

I **listen** to music at 4:00.

I **play** the piano at 5:30.

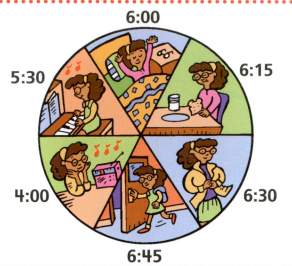

## Write.

1.

I eat dinner _____ at 5:30.

2.

_____
_____ at 10:30.

3.

_____
_____ at 4:45.

4.

_____
_____ at 5:15.

5.

_____
_____ at 6:30.

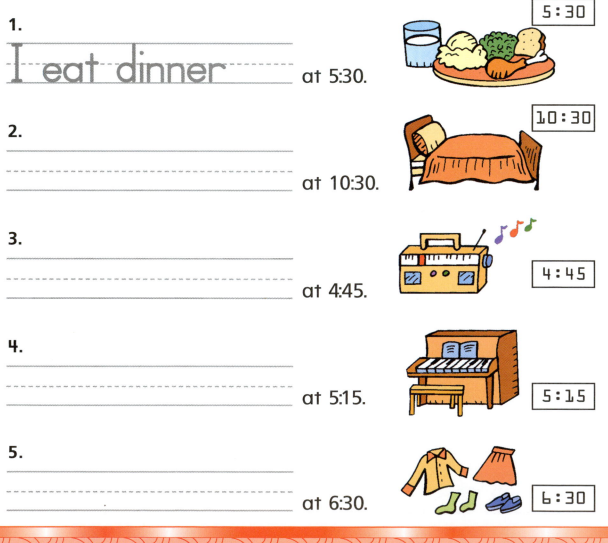

# Simple Present

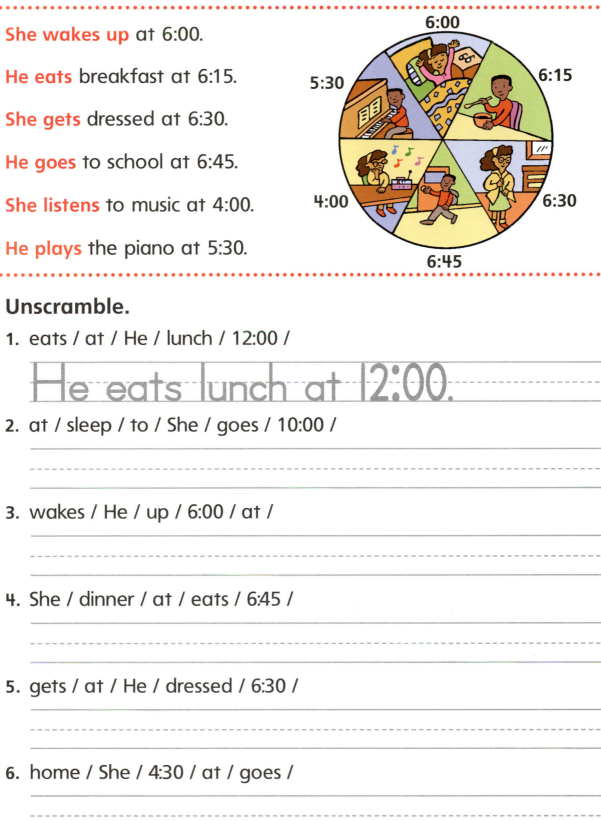

**She wakes up** at 6:00.

**He eats** breakfast at 6:15.

**She gets** dressed at 6:30.

**He goes** to school at 6:45.

**She listens** to music at 4:00.

**He plays** the piano at 5:30.

## Unscramble.

1. eats / at / He / lunch / 12:00 /

   He eats lunch at 12:00.

2. at / sleep / to / She / goes / 10:00 /

3. wakes / He / up / 6:00 / at /

4. She / dinner / at / eats / 6:45 /

5. gets / at / He / dressed / 6:30 /

6. home / She / 4:30 / at / goes /

## A. Match.

1. eat breakfast

2. go to sleep

3. get dressed

4. play the piano

5. listen to music

6. wake up

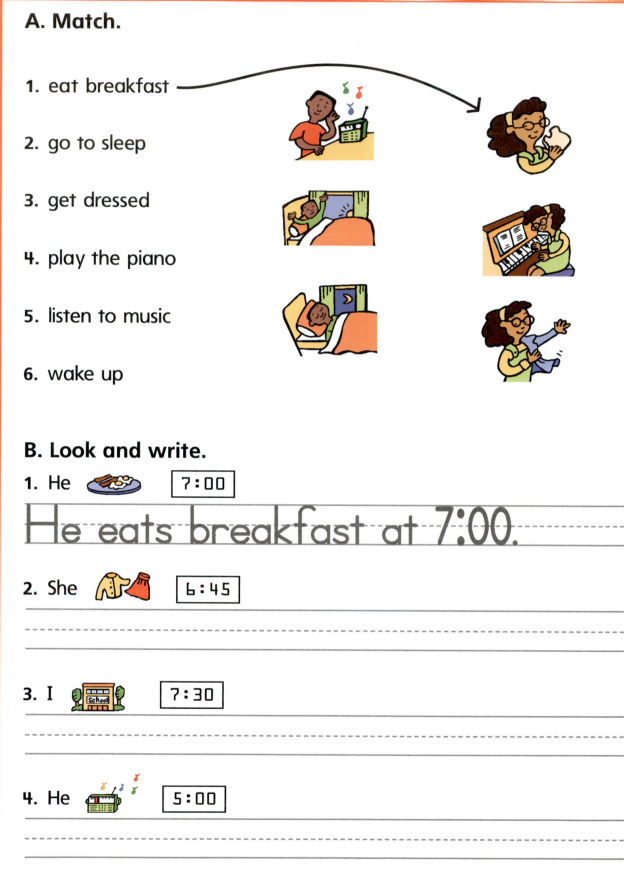

## B. Look and write.

1. He 🍳 | 7:00 |

He eats breakfast at 7:00.

2. She 👕👗 | 6:45 |

_____

- - - - - - - - - - - - - - - - -

_____

3. I 🏫 | 7:30 |

_____

- - - - - - - - - - - - - - - - -

_____

4. He 📻 | 5:00 |

_____

- - - - - - - - - - - - - - - - -

_____

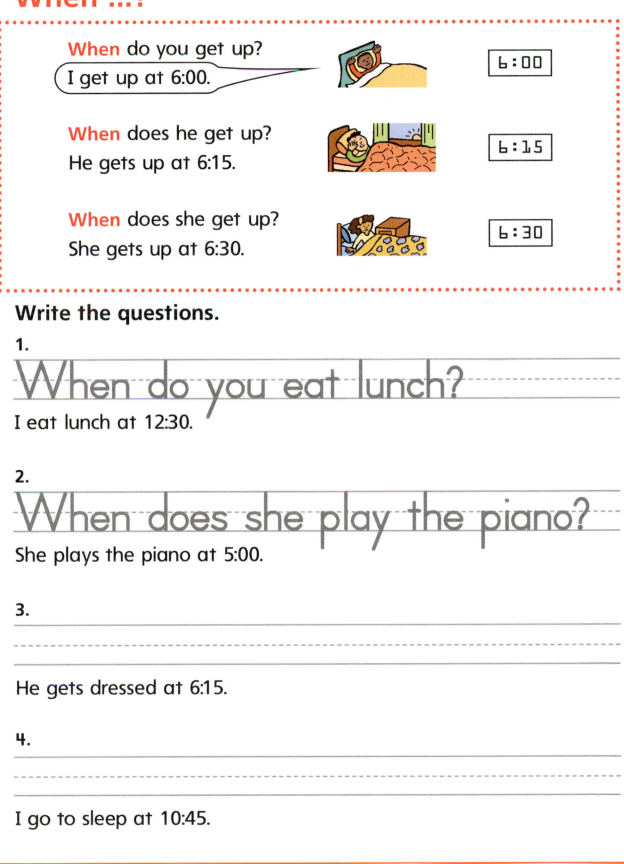

# When ...?

When do you get up?
I get up at 6:00.

6:00

When does he get up?
He gets up at 6:15.

6:15

When does she get up?
She gets up at 6:30.

6:30

**Write the questions.**

**1.**

When do you eat lunch?

I eat lunch at 12:30.

**2.**

When does she play the piano?

She plays the piano at 5:00.

**3.**

_____

He gets dressed at 6:15.

**4.**

_____

I go to sleep at 10:45.

**Write.**

My Day

1. I wake up at _____ .

2. _____

3. _____

4. _____

5. _____

6. _____

**Chant.**

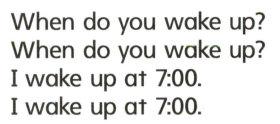

When do you wake up?
When do you wake up?
I wake up at 7:00.
I wake up at 7:00.

When do you get dressed?
When do you get dressed?
I get dressed at 7:30.
I get dressed at 7:30.

When do you eat lunch?
When do you eat lunch?
I eat lunch at 1:00.
I eat lunch at 1:00.

# A. Look and say.

wake up

play the piano

go to school

eat lunch

get dressed

go to sleep

# B. Write the words.

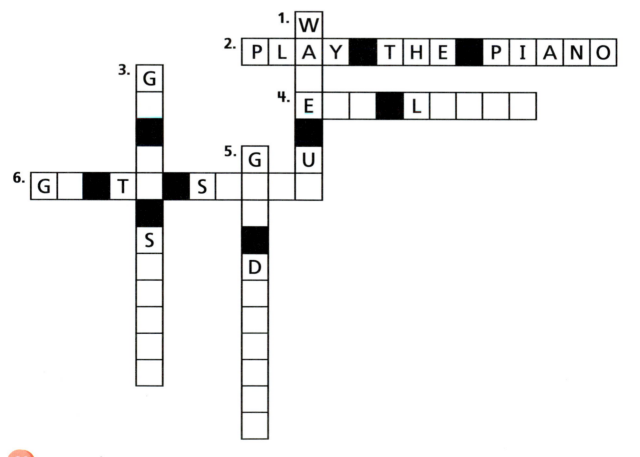

# Review: Units 5 and 6

## Vocabulary

🎧 **A. Listen and check.**

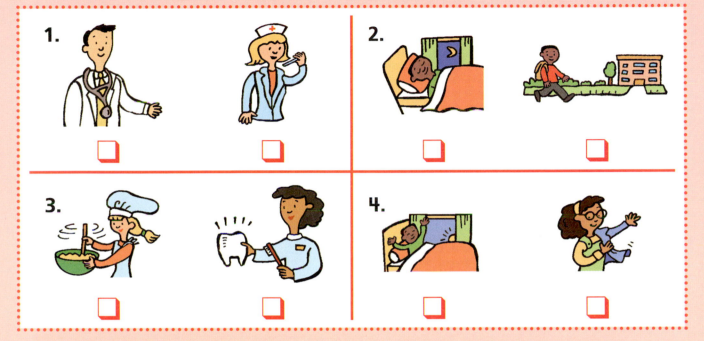

## What...?

🎧 **B. Listen and check.**

1. yes ☐ no ☐
2. yes ☐ no ☐
3. yes ☐ no ☐
4. yes ☐ no ☐
5. yes ☐ no ☐
6. yes ☐ no ☐

# Review: Units 5 and 6

## Simple Present

🎧 C. Listen and check.

## Simple Present

🎧 D. Listen, point, and say.

# Food

potato

fish

water

onion

bread

tomato

carrot

orange

cheese

rice

chicken

mango

soup

# Plural Nouns

Many plural nouns end in **-s.**

I want a carrot.     I want three carrot**s.**

Some plural nouns end in **-es.**

tomato**es**
potato**es**

## Write.

**1.** I want an onion.

I want three onions.
(three)

**2.** I want an orange.

(three)

**3.** I want a tomato.

I want four tomatoes.
(four)

**4.** I want a potato.

(three)

# Noncount Nouns

Some nouns can be counted.

I want **three potatoes**.

Some nouns cannot be counted. They do not have a plural form.

I want **some chicken**.

**Write.**

**1.**

I want some water.

(water)

**2.**

_____

_____

(bread)

**3.**

_____

_____

(rice)

**Write.**

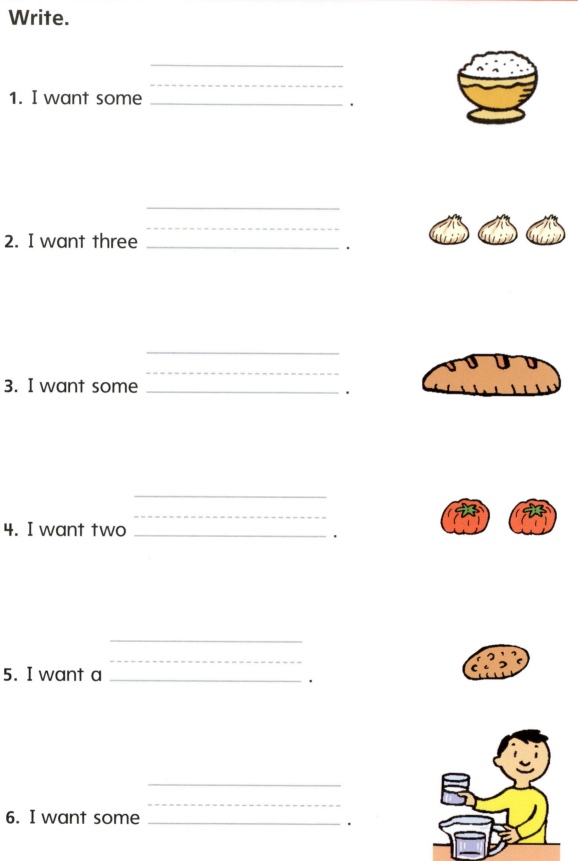

1. I want some _____ .

2. I want three _____ .

3. I want some _____ .

4. I want two _____ .

5. I want a _____ .

6. I want some _____ .

# Some

Use **some** with plural nouns and noncount nouns.

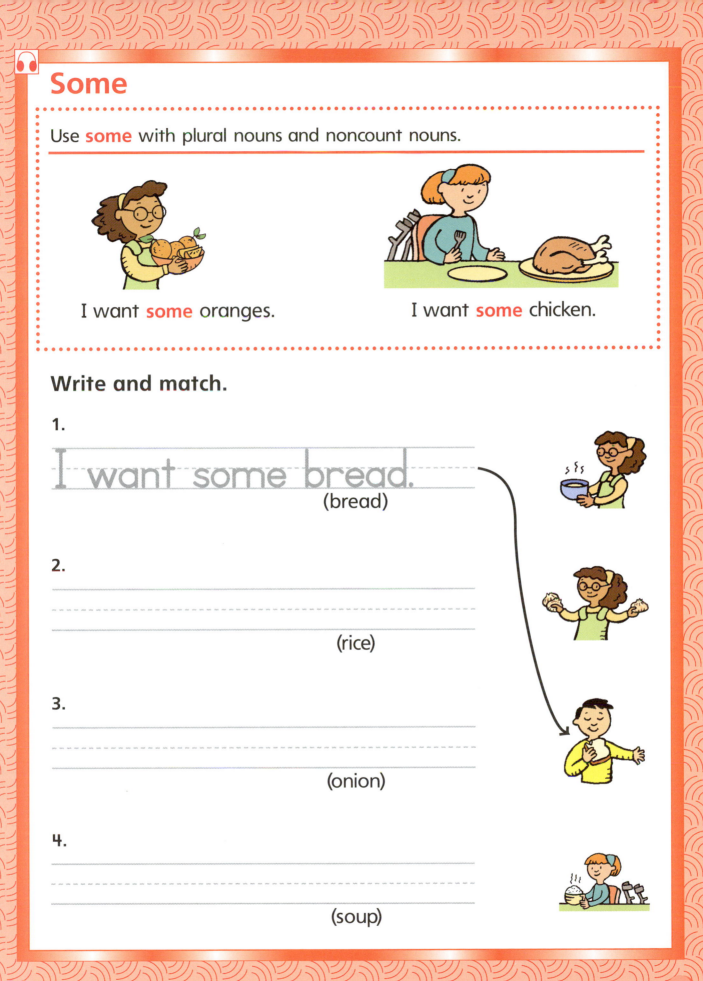

I want **some** oranges.

I want **some** chicken.

## Write and match.

1.

I want some bread.

(bread)

2.

_____

(rice)

3.

_____

(onion)

4.

_____

(soup)

## Read and draw.

1. There is some bread on the table.

2. There are three oranges on the table.

3. There is some cheese on the table.

4. There are five tomatoes on the table.

5. There is some fish on the table.

6. There is an onion on the table.

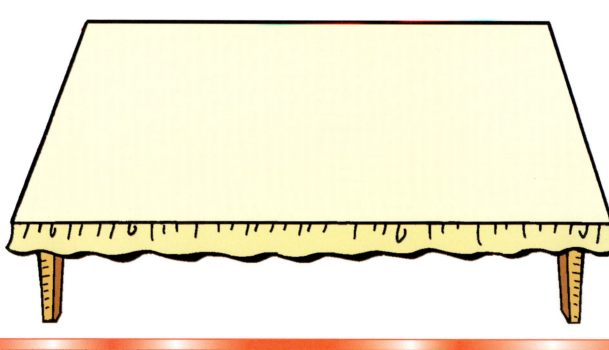

Cheese, cheese
I want some cheese.

Rice, rice
I want some rice.

Soup, soup
I want some soup.

Mangoes, mangoes
I want some mangoes.

Onions, onions
I want some onions.

Carrots, carrots
I want some carrots.

# Find the words.

oranges

water

cheese

onion

carrots

chicken

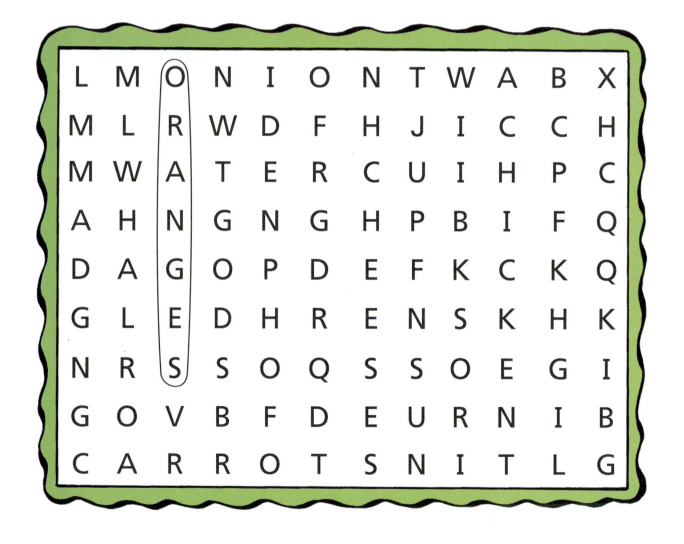

L M O N I O N T W A B X
M L R W D F H J I C C H
M W A T E R C U I H P C
A H N G N G H P B I F Q
D A G O P D E F K C K Q
G L E D H R E N S K H K
N R S S O Q S S O E G I
G O V B F D E U R N I B
C A R R O T S N I T L G

# At the Zoo

elephant

gorilla

alligator

hippo

lion

monkey

seal

zebra

bear

tiger

panda

giraffe

# Punctuation: Exclamation Mark

Look at the lion**!**

## Write and draw.

1.

(gorilla)

2.

_____
- - - - - - - - - - - - - -
_____
(bear)

3.

_____
- - - - - - - - - - - - - -
_____
(tiger)

4.

_____
- - - - - - - - - - - - - -
_____
(panda)

5.

_____
- - - - - - - - - - - - - -
_____
(hippo)

# Have/Has

What does an elephant **have**?

An elephant **has** a long trunk.

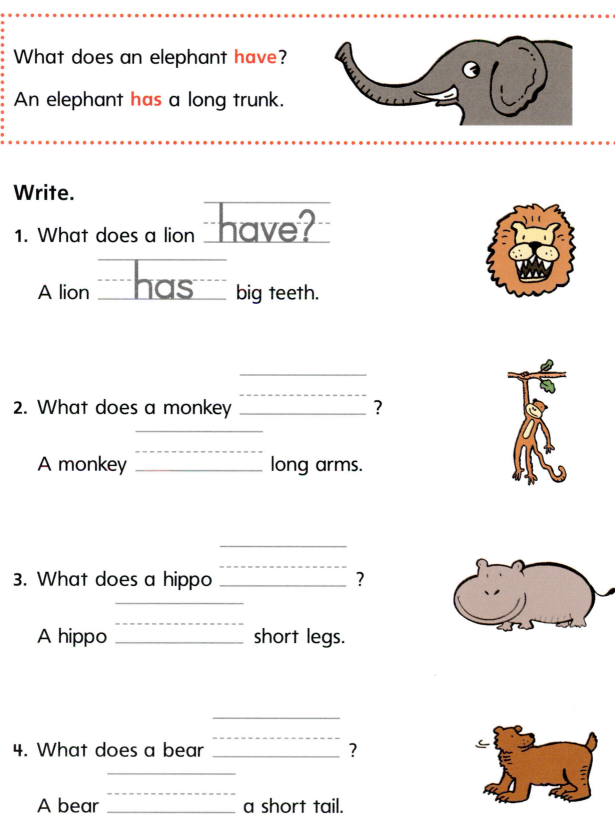

**Write.**

1. What does a lion have?

   A lion has big teeth.

2. What does a monkey _____ ?

   A monkey _____ long arms.

3. What does a hippo _____ ?

   A hippo _____ short legs.

4. What does a bear _____ ?

   A bear _____ a short tail.

**Write.**

1. What does an alligator _have_ ?

An alligator has a long tail.                    long tail

2. What does a tiger _____ ?

_____        big teeth

3. What does a panda _____ ?

_____        small ears

4. What does a gorilla _____ ?

_____        long arms

5. What does a giraffe _____ ?

_____        long neck

# Its/Their

The alligator's tail is long.

**Its** tail is long.

The lions' teeth are big.

**Their** teeth are big.

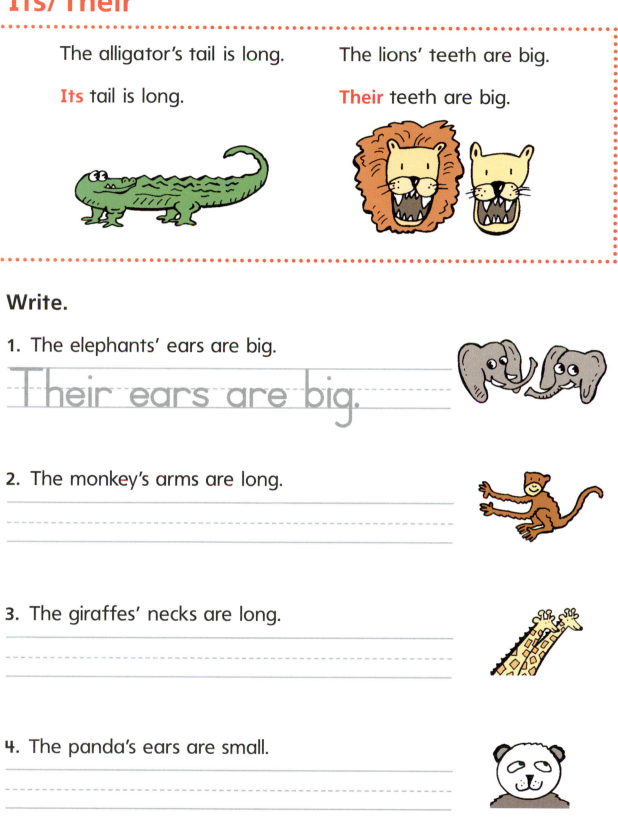

## Write.

1. The elephants' ears are big.

Their ears are big.

2. The monkey's arms are long.

3. The giraffes' necks are long.

4. The panda's ears are small.

**Draw.**

1. Its teeth are big.

2. Its tail is long.

3. Its ears are big.

4. Its tail is short.

5. Its mouth is big.

 **Chant.**

Its teeth are big.
Its teeth are big.
It's a lion!
It's a lion!

Its ears are small.
Its ears are small.
It's a bear!
It's a bear!

Its arms are long.
Its arms are long.
It's a monkey!
It's a monkey!

Its mouth is big.
Its mouth is big.
It's a hippo!
It's a hippo!

# Find and color.

giraffe     elephant     hippo     alligator     gorilla     bear

# Review: Units 7 and 8

## Vocabulary

A. Listen and check.

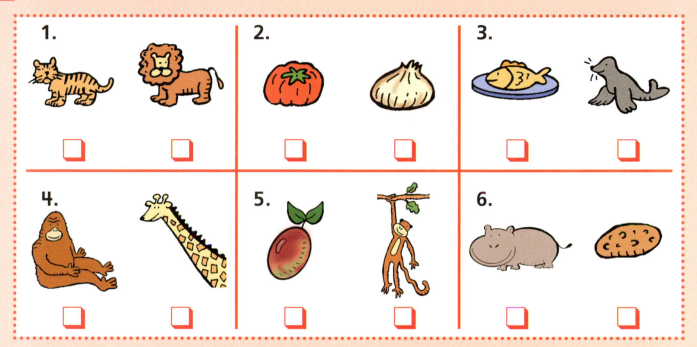

## Singular and Plural Nouns

B. Listen and check.

# Review: Units 7 and 8

## Its/Their

C. Listen and check.

1.

yes ☐   no ☐

2.

yes ☐   no ☐

3.

yes ☐   no ☐

4.

yes ☐   no ☐

5.

yes ☐   no ☐

6.

yes ☐   no ☐

## Have/Has

D. Listen, point, and say.

1.

2.

3.

4.

5.

6.

# Celebrations

visit family

give presents

wear a mask

send cards

dance in a parade

watch fireworks

make a wish

# Always/Never

Always = 100%       Never = 0%

We **always** watch fireworks on New Year's Day.

We **never** watch fireworks on New Year's Day.

**Write.**

1. We _always_ dance in a parade on New Year's Day.

2. We _never_ dance in a parade on New Year's Day.

3. We _____ give presents on holidays.

4. We _____ give presents on holidays.

# Sometimes

**Sometimes** = 50%

I **sometimes** visit friends on holidays.

## Draw and write.

I sometimes _____ on holidays.

**Write about you.**

1. I _____ give presents on holidays.
   (always   sometimes   never)

2. I _____ dance in a parade on holidays.
   (always   sometimes   never)

3. I _____ watch fireworks on holidays.
   (always   sometimes   never)

4. I _____ wear a mask on holidays.
   (always   sometimes   never)

5. I _____ make a wish on holidays.
   (always   sometimes   never)

# When ...?

When is John's birthday?

His birthday is in March.

When is Maria's birthday?

Her birthday is in May.

**Write.**

1.

When is her birthday? (her)

Her birthday is in December.

2.

(his)

His birthday is in .

3.

(her)

Her birthday is in .

4.

(your)

My birthday is in .

**Circle and write.**

**My Family and Friends**

| January | February | March | April | May | June |
|---|---|---|---|---|---|
| | | | | | |

| July | August | September | October | November | December |
|---|---|---|---|---|---|
| | | | | | |

1. My father's birthday is in _____ .

2. My _____ .

3. _____

4. _____

5. _____

 **Chant.**

When is your birthday?

When is your birthday?

My birthday is in May.

My birthday is in May.


January, February, March,

April, May, June,

July, August, September,

October, November, December.

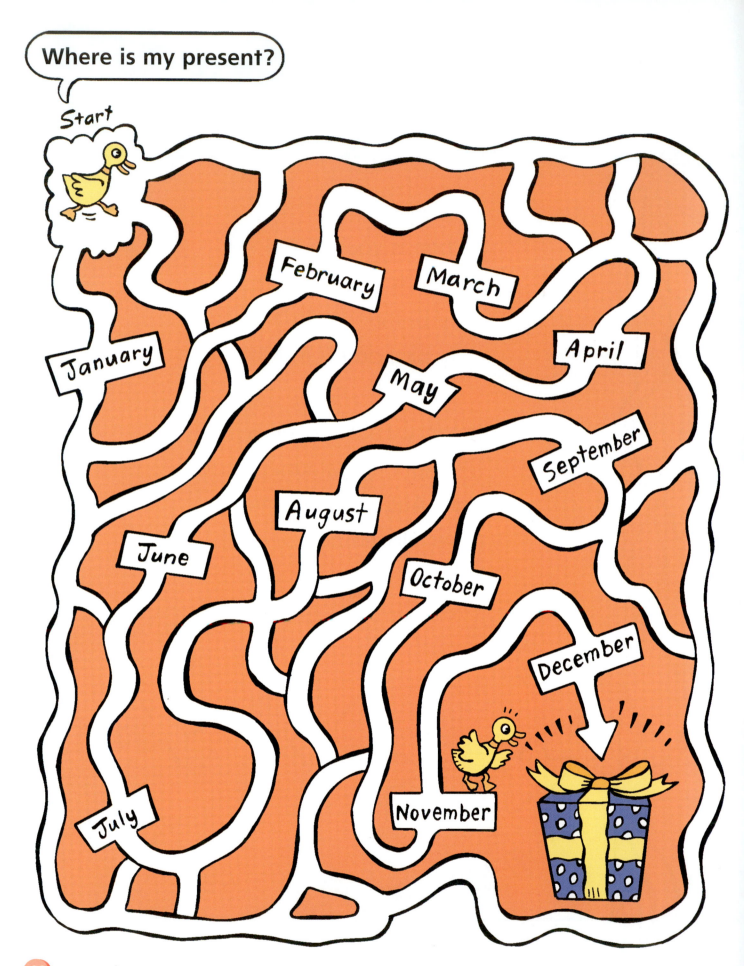

# Transformation

# How ...?

**How** do you go to school?

I go to school by car.

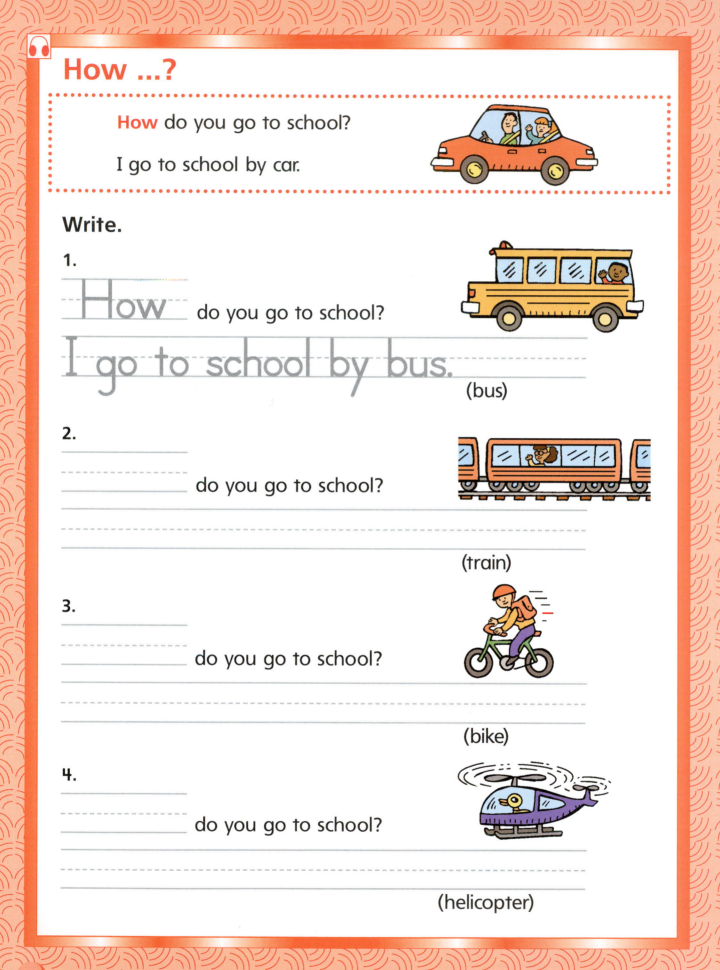

**Write.**

1.

How do you go to school?

I go to school by bus.

(bus)

2.

_____ do you go to school?

(train)

3.

_____ do you go to school?

(bike)

4.

_____ do you go to school?

(helicopter)

# How ...?

> **How** does she go to work?
>
> She goes to work by train.

**Write.**

**1.**

How does she go to work?
She goes to work by bus.
(bus)

**2.**

_____ does she go to work?

(boat)

**3.**

_____ does he go to work?

(subway)

**4.**

_____ does she go to work?

(car)

**Write.**

1. How does he go to school?

   He goes to school by bike .

   _____

2. _____ go to school?

   She _____ .

3. _____

   He _____ .

4. How does he go to work?

   He goes to work by train .

   _____

5. _____ go to work?

   She _____ .

6. _____

   He _____ .

# How are you feeling?

I'm happy.

I'm sad.

I'm tired.

I'm hungry.

I'm thirsty.

**Write.**

1. I'm _____ .

2. I'm _____ .

3. I'm _____ .

4. I'm _____ .

5. I'm _____ .

## A. Unscramble and circle.

1. pyaph  happy

2. dsa  _____

3. yhitsrt  _____

4. nhgyur  _____

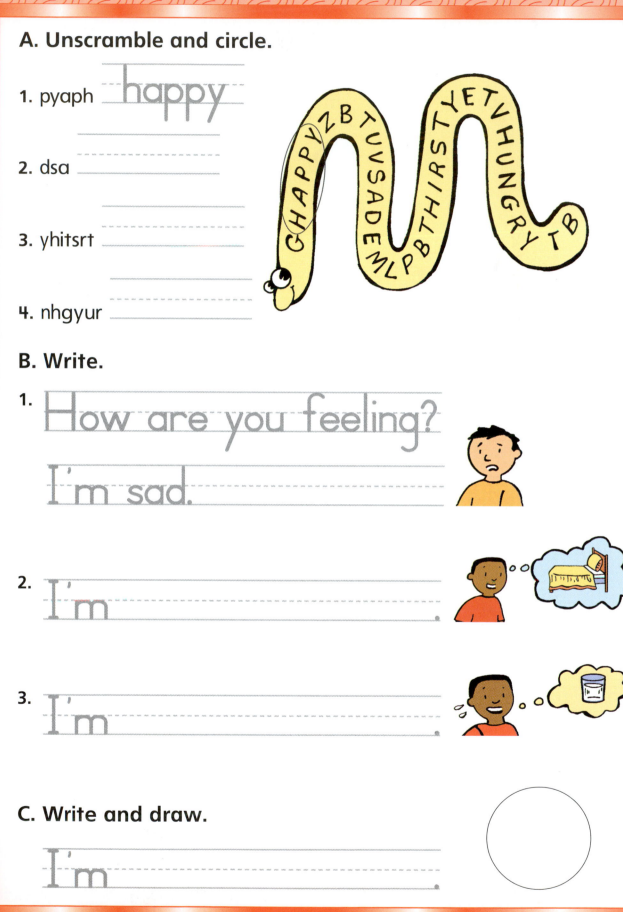

## B. Write.

1. How are you feeling?
   I'm sad.

2. I'm _____.

3. I'm _____.

## C. Write and draw.

I'm _____.

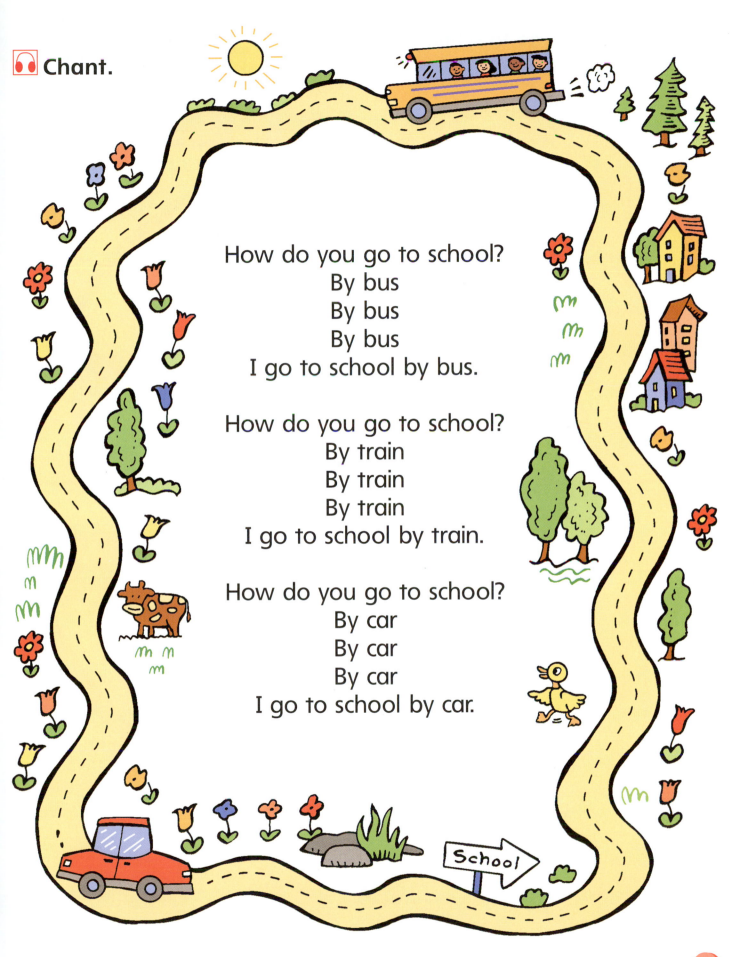

How do you go to school?
By bus
By bus
By bus
I go to school by bus.

How do you go to school?
By train
By train
By train
I go to school by train.

How do you go to school?
By car
By car
By car
I go to school by car.

School

# How do you go to school?

Drop a paper clip onto an object in the circle.

# Review: Units 9 and 10

## Vocabulary
A. Listen and check.

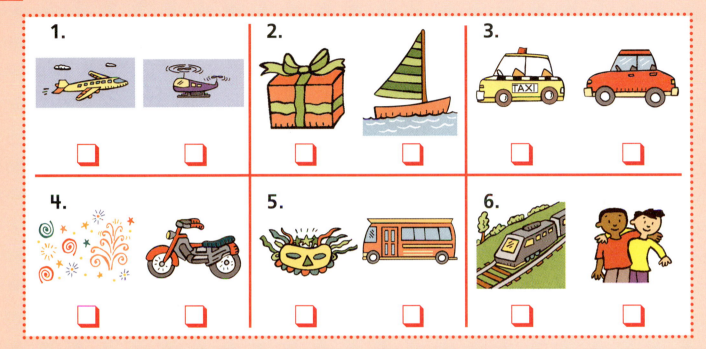

## Always/Never
B. Listen and check.

# Review: Units 9 and 10

## How...?

🎧 **C. Listen and check.**

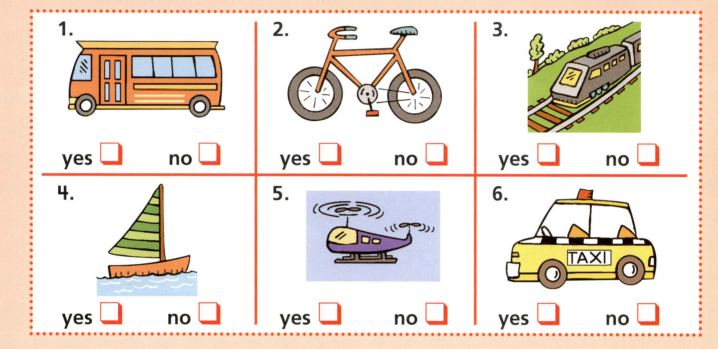

| 1. | 2. | 3. |
|---|---|---|
| yes ☐    no ☐ | yes ☐    no ☐ | yes ☐    no ☐ |
| 4. | 5. | 6. |
| yes ☐    no ☐ | yes ☐    no ☐ | yes ☐    no ☐ |

## How are you feeling?

🎧 **D. Listen, point, and say.**

1.

2.

3.

4.

# Numbers and Shapes Practice

## A. Write the number.

1. forty-two    42

2. twenty-three

3. fourteen

4. seventy-five

5. fifty-one

6. three

7. thirty-six

8. sixty-four

9. ninety

10. one hundred

## B. Draw the shape.

1. triangle

2. rectangle

3. circle

4. heart

5. square

6. star

# Seasons and Time Practice

**Draw.**

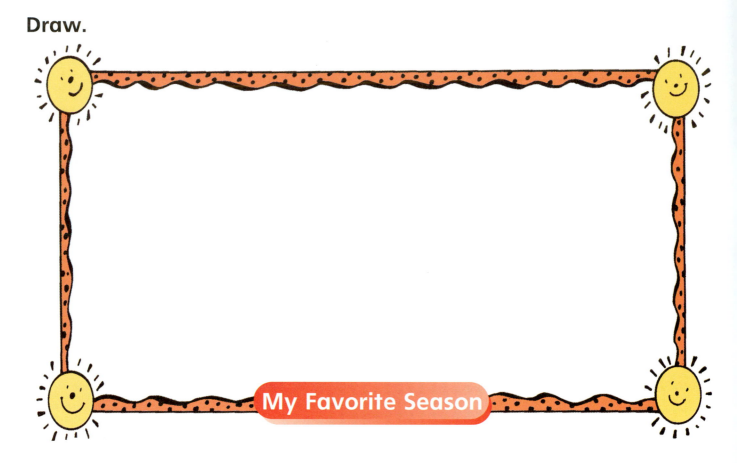

My Favorite Season

**Fill in the clocks.**

**1.** four thirty

**2.** three forty-five

**3.** twelve o'clock

**4.** two fifteen

**5.** one ten

**6.** ten twenty

**Draw your picture. Write your name.**

Hello! My name is _____ .

# Word List

above

airplane

alligator

ant

bakery

bank

bear

behind

bench

between

big

bike

boat

bookstore

bread

bus

butterfly

cloud

car

computer

card

cook

carrot

cut

cheese

dance

chicken

dentist

clerk

doctor

close

door

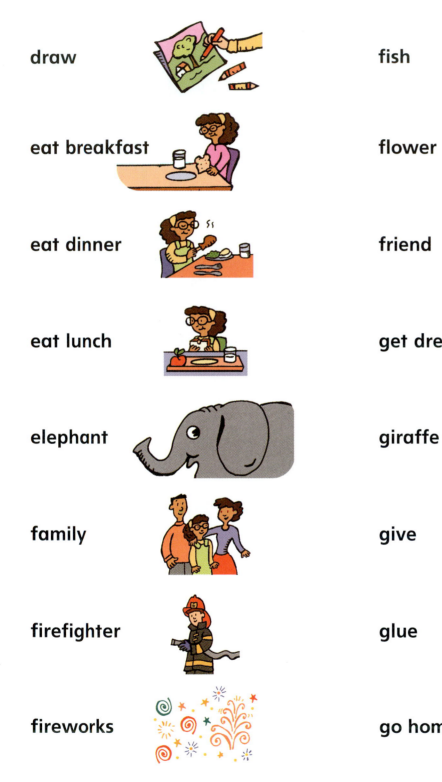

draw

eat breakfast

eat dinner

eat lunch

elephant

family

firefighter

fireworks

fish

flower

friend

get dressed

giraffe

give

glue

go home

go to school

go to sleep

gorilla

happy

helicopter

hippo

hospital

house

hungry

librarian

library

lion

listen to music

mail carrier

make a wish

mango

| | | | |
|---|---|---|---|
| mask |  | old | |
| mirror | | on | |
| monkey | | onion | |
| motorcycle | | open | |
| new | | orange | |
| next to | | panda | |
| notebook | | paper | |
| nurse | | parade | |

pet

play the piano

police officer

post office

potato

present

radio

restaurant

rice

rug

sad

scissors

seal

seesaw

send

short

sink

small

soup

squirrel

subway

sun

supermarket

swing

tall

taxi

teacher

telephone

thirsty

tiger

tomato

train

tree

vet

visit

wake up

watch

water

wear

window

zebra